When the Earth Shakes

By Charles Higgins and Regina Higgins

Modern Curriculum Press
Parsippany, New Jersey

Credits

Photos:

Front Cover: Reuters/John Pryke/Archive Photos. Title page: Reuters Newsmedia Inc./Corbis/Bettmann. 5: Reuters Newsmedia Inc./Corbis/Bettmann. 6: Laura Riley/Bruce Coleman Inc. 7: ©David Weintraub/Photo Researchers, Inc. 8: Leverett Bradley/Stone Images. 10: U. S. Army. 11: Gerry Ellis/ENP Images. 16: ©Wesley Bocxe/Photo Researchers, Inc. 17: AP/Wide World Photos. 18: ©Joe Sohm/Photo Researchers, Inc. 19: Corbis-Bettmann. 21: Bob Rowan/Progressive Images/Corbis. 23: Corbis-Bettmann. 24: ©Krafft/Hoa-Qui/Photo Researchers, Inc. 25: Corbis-Bettmann. 27: Bill Thompson/Earth Images. 28: Stone Images. 29: Reuters/Kimimasa Mayama/Archive Photos. 31: Reuters Newsmedia Inc./Corbis. 32: Michael S. Yamashita/Corbis. 33: ©Wesley Bocxe/Photo Researchers, Inc. 34: AFP/Corbis. 35: Reuters Newsmedia Inc./Corbis. 36: Mitch York/Stone Images. 38: James Balog/Stone Images. 39: David Falconer/Bruce Coleman Inc. 40: ©Ken M. Johns/Photo Researchers, Inc. 42: David Madison/Bruce Coleman Inc. 43: Anne Keiser/National Geographic Society. 45: James Stanfield/National Geographic Society. 46: David Hanson/Stone Images. 47: Reuters Newsmedia Inc./Corbis.

Illustrations:

12–13: Mapping Specialists Ltd. 14, 15: P.T. Pie Illustrations. 20: Mapping Specialists Ltd. 26: P.T. Pie Illustrations.

Cover and Book design by Stephen Barth

Modern Curriculum Press

An imprint of Pearson Learning
299 Jefferson Road, P.O. Box 480
Parsippany, NJ 07054-0480

w w w.pearsonlearning.com

1-800-321-3106

ISBN 0-7652-2157-8

8 9 10 V031 17 16 15 14

Modern Curriculum Press

Contents

For Frances and Charles—
Earth shakers!

Chapter 1

It's an Earthquake!

A woman and her children watched as the water in their swimming pool suddenly spouted five feet in the air. A man watched cars in a parking lot hop around as if they were toys. A woman went to sleep with her bed against one wall in her bedroom. The bed was against another wall when she woke up.

A parking lot and building are destroyed by an earthquake.

A boy and his dad were in their car. It suddenly started to bounce, as if there were big bumps in the road. The road itself bent and twisted. The broken concrete slabs dipped and rolled like the waves of an ocean.

These people were experiencing earthquakes. An earthquake is a sudden shaking of the earth's surface. The tremors can be so mild that they barely make leaves on a tree flutter. They can be so violent that they cause cracks in the earth hundreds of miles long.

Damage from the 1994 Los Angeles earthquake

Rescuers look for people after an earthquake in San Francisco.

Major earthquakes can cause great destruction. The most serious problems happen when buildings collapse. People inside can be trapped.

After an earthquake is over, the danger and damage may still go on. The water in damaged pipes below the street may burst out like a fountain. Whole sections of a city may be flooded. The roads and streets themselves may crack open. When that happens emergency crews cannot reach people who need help.

When gas pipelines under the street break, the leaking gas can start fires. If water pipes are broken, firefighters may be unable to get water to put out the flames.

Cities are not the only places damaged by earthquakes. In hilly areas, loose rock and soil tumble down hillsides when the ground shakes. The landslide becomes a mudslide if the ground has been soaked by rain.

In areas with lots of snow, the shaking ground causes snow and ice to roll down hillsides. Like a landslide or mudslide, an avalanche crushes everything it reaches.

After an earthquake, a landslide
caused more damage to this house.

Sometimes a small earthquake can cause more damage than a large one. It depends on where the earthquake happens. This makes comparing the size of earthquakes difficult.

The Richter scale is the system most people use to compare earthquakes. This scale tells how much the ground shakes at any point 60 miles away from the epicenter of the earthquake. The epicenter is the point in the ground where the earthquake starts.

The Richter scale goes from 1 to 9. The number 1 means an earthquake too small for people to feel. The number 9 is the strongest earthquake. Each step on the Richter scale is for an earthquake ten times stronger than the last step. So an earthquake measuring 7 is ten times stronger than one registering 6. It usually takes an earthquake registering between 5 and 6 to damage homes. Major earthquakes are any that measure over 7. An earthquake that measures as high as 8 on the Richter scale is rare. There has never been an earthquake recorded as high as 9.

Scientists measure the movements of the ground with an instrument called a seismograph. How much the ground moves is shown on a computer or on paper as jagged lines that go up and down. A strong earthquake will be recorded with big jagged lines.

About 500,000 or more earthquakes happen every year around the world. Most of these earthquakes are very small. About 5,000 of the earthquakes are big enough for people to feel. About 1,000 of them are strong enough to cause some damage.

Anchorage, Alaska, after the 1964 earthquake

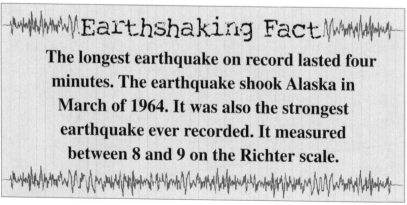

⩩⩩⩩Earthshaking Fact⩩⩩⩩

The longest earthquake on record lasted four minutes. The earthquake shook Alaska in March of 1964. It was also the strongest earthquake ever recorded. It measured between 8 and 9 on the Richter scale.

Chapter 2

How Earthquakes Happen

In ancient times, many people made up myths, or stories, to explain why the earth shakes. Native Americans living in California told the tale of six turtles who supported the world on their backs. The Great Spirit told the turtles not to move. When the turtles argued, they tried to move away from each other. The earth shook when they moved.

Rock drawing of a turtle

People in California and all over the world now know that earthquakes are caused by movements within the earth. These powerful movements come from deep within the earth. They travel upward to the earth's surface where people can feel them. To understand how these movements shake the earth's surface, think of the earth as having several layers instead of being a solid ball.

Earth's tectonic plates

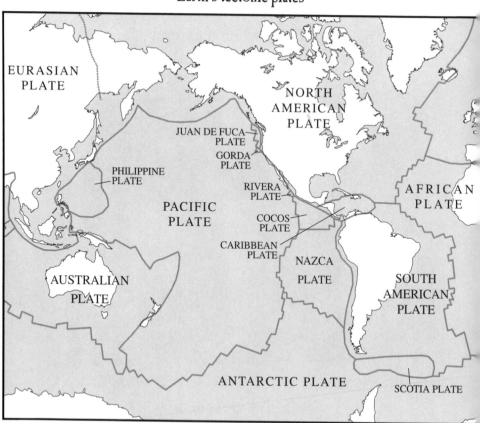

The outer layer, or crust, is hard and rocky. It is like a shell that is about 70 miles thick. Unlike a shell, though, the crust is not smooth. It is in pieces that fit together like a jigsaw puzzle. These pieces are called tectonic plates. Every ocean and continent lies on a tectonic plate that is part of the earth's crust.

The earth's crust rests on another layer. It is called the mantle, which is a mass of partly melted rock. The melted rock is called magma. It is soft, gooey, and very hot. As the magma moves, the tectonic plates move, too.

The plates on the mantle move very, very slowly. The plate that holds North America and the plate that holds Europe, for example, are moving apart at the rate of four inches per year. This is too slow for people to see or feel.

EURASIAN PLATE

ARABIAN PLATE

PHILIPPINE PLATE

INDIAN PLATE

SOMALI PLATE

AUSTRALIAN PLATE

—— Plate boundary

········ Indefinite plate boundary

ANTARCTIC PLATE

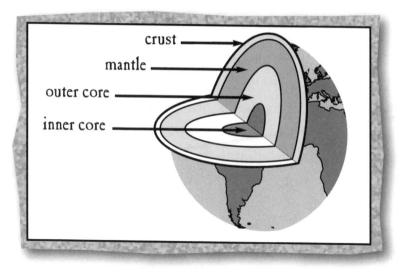

The layers of the earth

Beneath the mantle lies the outer core. At the very center is the inner core, a ball of solid rock. The inner and outer cores are very hot. Scientists think that temperatures in the inner core may reach 9,000 degrees Fahrenheit. The heat from the core acts like a furnace to keep the magma soft and constantly moving.

The plates move easily unless two plates meet and try to push past or under each other. The edges of the plates can stick together when they meet. The magma underneath the plates keeps moving. This forces the plates together even harder.

The plates can stay stuck for hundreds or even thousands of years. Then suddenly, the plates jolt past each other. This movement of the earth's crust causes an earthquake.

14

After the first sudden movement, the plates may move a little more. These later movements cause more shaking and are called aftershocks. Aftershocks can occur hours, days, weeks, or even months after the first big earthquake. Usually, the later the aftershocks come, the smaller they are.

The point under the ground where the plates shift is called the focus. The focus can be more than 400 miles below the earth's surface. This is where the earthquake begins and where its force is the most powerful.

The vibrations that start at the focus move upward at a rate of up to ten miles per second. The spot above the focus on the earth's surface is the epicenter. The most destruction happens at the epicenter during an earthquake.

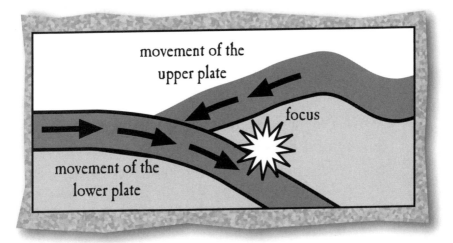

Where an earthquake happens

After an earthquake in Mexico City

There are places on Earth that are much more likely than others to have major earthquakes. These places sit above the point where the edges of tectonic plates meet. Skyscrapers, homes, highways, and even sports arenas have all been built in such places. Sometimes they are built to withstand an earthquake. Sometimes they are not.

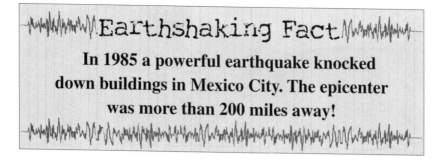

Earthshaking Fact

In 1985 a powerful earthquake knocked down buildings in Mexico City. The epicenter was more than 200 miles away!

Chapter 3

Living on the Edge

In the afternoon of October 17, 1989, baseball fans filled San Francisco's Candlestick Park. They were excited for the start of the third game of the World Series between the San Francisco Giants and the Oakland Athletics.

Suddenly, there was a rumbling across the field. The bleachers shook. Blocks of concrete fell from the stadium's balconies. San Francisco was having an earthquake!

Players help people after the earthquake in Candlestick Park.

17

Collapsed highway in San Francisco, 1989

Amazingly, no one in Candlestick Park was seriously hurt by the earthquake. The worst damage was in West Oakland across San Francisco Bay.

The earthquake struck at 5:04 P.M. The roadways were packed with cars. One highway fell on top of another. Many people were trapped in their cars, and some died.

The 1989 earthquake measured 6.4 on the Richter scale. This was not the first time San Francisco had experienced an earthquake. The same area had suffered a bigger, more serious earthquake 83 years earlier.

Early one April morning in 1906, a terrible earthquake shook San Francisco. It measured 7.7 on the Richter scale. Buildings tumbled into rubble in less than two minutes. The streets cracked open. People fled their houses in a panic. Many others were trapped in the fallen buildings.

The damage that came after the earthquake was even worse. Gas lamps and stoves caused fires when they fell over. Underground gas pipes also burst. Fire spread all over the city. It took three days to put out all the fires. Over 28,000 buildings burned to the ground. The earthquake and its fires killed nearly 2,500 people.

After the San Francisco earthquake in 1906

San Francisco's two major earthquakes were not unusual for that part of the country. California has more earthquakes than any other part of the United States. This is because San Francisco lies just at the meeting point of two tectonic plates. These are the Pacific Plate and the North American Plate.

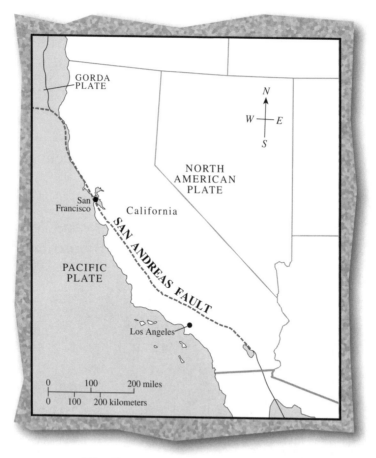

The San Andreas Fault in California

As seen from above, the San Andreas Fault looks like a large crack in the ground.

Where the plates meet is called the San Andreas Fault. A fault is a crack in the earth's surface, usually between two tectonic plates. The San Andreas Fault runs nearly the whole length of California. It passes under San Francisco and very near Los Angeles. The San Andreas Fault causes many of the earthquakes in California.

There are also smaller fault lines in California. After the 1987 earthquake in Los Angeles, scientists discovered six fault lines under the city. Any of these faults, together with the San Andreas Fault, can cause an earthquake.

The entire coast around the Pacific Ocean, including California, has many earthquakes. Look back at the map on pages 12 and 13. This area includes the Pacific Plate, the Nazca Plate, and the Australian Plate. The coasts of North and South America, Japan, and islands in the western Pacific are also in this region. About three out of four earthquakes in the world occur here.

Earthshaking Fact

One California fault is the San Gabriel Fault.
It lies in the area in which Native Americans long
ago told stories about the earth trembling
when the turtles argued. Earthquakes
must have happened often there.

Chapter 4

Tsunamis and Volcanoes

One of the strongest earthquakes ever recorded began in Chile and rumbled all around the Pacific Ocean in May of 1960. Damage extended from Chile to California, Alaska, Hawaii, and even Japan.

The fault running along the coast of Chile moved in several jolts. The largest earthquake measured 8.3 on the Richter scale. Aftershocks caused more earthquakes within hours.

Damage in a Japanese harbor in 1960 after an earthquake caused large ocean waves

Valdivia, Chile, is built on a fault. The city trembled and sank almost seven feet as the tectonic plate jolted into a new position. The earthquakes caused rock slides in Chile's Andes Mountains. Two days after the first earthquake, a volcano erupted from one of the mountains. Burning lava poured down the mountainside.

Volcano in Chile

Damage after a tsunami in Hawaii

After the earthquakes, ocean waves grew enormous in places all around the Pacific Ocean. These waves are called tsunamis (soo NAHM eez). They flooded areas of the Hawaiian Islands 20 feet deep. The waves that hit the shore crushed buildings. Many homes, cars, and heavy machinery were washed away. In Japan, waves surged 20 feet inland. In California, waves reached more than 250 feet inland in one spot.

How could there be earthquakes, enormous ocean waves, and volcanoes all happening at the same time? The same movements in the earth's crust that cause earthquakes can cause volcanoes and tsunamis, too.

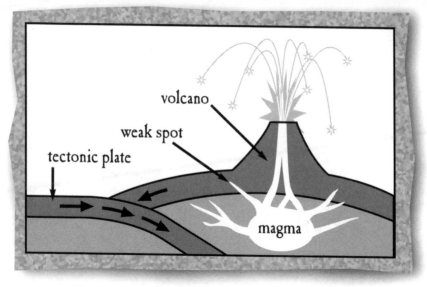

How a volcano forms

Most volcanoes in the world are located along the same fault lines where earthquakes happen, especially in the countries around the Pacific Ocean. That's why this area is often called the Ring of Fire.

A fault line between tectonic plates creates a lot of weak spots in the crust. The hot, liquid magma under the earth's crust seeps into these cracks or weak spots. The magma can push the crust up in a point, forming a volcanic mountain. The formation of this mountain can take hundreds or even thousands of years.

The magma is mixed with explosive bubbly gases. So, when the magma finally breaks through the mountain, it often explodes. The fiery magma shoots out of the mountaintop, spraying red-hot liquid and rock all around. A volcano is born!

26

When magma pours out onto the earth's surface, it is called lava. Lava is fiery hot. The lava that pours down a volcano's mountainsides burns everything in its path.

The tiny bits of lava that shoot up in an explosion cool as they hit the air, like sparks from a campfire. As the bits fall, they cover the ground and everything else with volcanic ash.

A man washes volcanic ash from a car after the eruption of Mount St. Helens in Washington in 1980

Volcanoes can also create new land. Volcanoes form and erupt where plates are spreading apart. Lava from the underwater volcanoes fills in the crack between the spreading plates. This is happening in the Atlantic Ocean.

The Hawaiian Islands in the Pacific Ocean were formed by volcanoes in a different way. One hot spot of magma in the earth's mantle pushed magma up through the crust. This action formed a volcano that poked above the water. The crust moved very slowly over the hot spot. A line of volcanic islands formed as the crust moved.

The Hawaiian Islands were formed by volcanoes long ago.

Damage after an earthquake and tsunami in Japan in 1993

Tsunamis are formed when an earthquake happens on the ocean floor. The powerful tremors shake the water in the same way that an earthquake on land shakes the surrounding area.

Small waves begin to form on the surface as the water shakes. The waves get larger and larger as the shaking continues. Some tsunamis tower nearly 100 feet high by the time they reach land. These powerful waves can also be hundreds of miles wide.

Tsunamis travel quickly and can hit a coast suddenly. They can move at a speed of 500 miles per hour. This is as fast as a jet plane. Waves may repeatedly pound the shore for hours. They knock down buildings, rip up beaches, and flood the whole area.

Japan is one country that has been hit by many tsunamis and earthquakes. The Japanese have learned from their experience with these monster waves and earthquakes. They are becoming experts at rescuing people trapped by floods, in crumbled buildings, and by fallen rock.

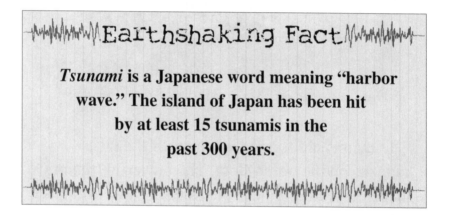

Earthshaking Fact

Tsunami is a Japanese word meaning "harbor wave." The island of Japan has been hit by at least 15 tsunamis in the past 300 years.

Chapter 5

Earthquake Rescues

People rush to try to help others who are hurt or trapped in collapsed buildings after an earthquake or tsunami hits. They have to be careful. The possibility of aftershocks means the possibility of more damage. Loose parts of buildings may fall. Only specially trained rescue workers may go into damaged areas. This work is very dangerous, but it is the only way to save people's lives.

Japanese rescue workers check for survivors.

Rescuers look for earthquake survivors at the Kobe train station.

Trained rescuers travel around the world to help where earthquakes and other disasters have occurred. The American Rescue Team International, ARTI, has been at most major disasters since 1985.

A major earthquake in 1995 hit Kobe, one of Japan's largest cities. ARTI was there. This earthquake registered 7.2 on the Richter scale and lasted only 20 seconds. The damage was the worst Japan had seen in over 70 years. Nearly 180,000 buildings collapsed or were badly damaged.

The train station in Kobe collapsed with people inside. The ARTI rescuers crawled into spaces with as little as one-and-a-half feet of headroom. Sometimes they had to crawl like this for hundreds of feet, looking for survivors.

Rescuers also use special equipment to help find people trapped in buildings or by fallen rock. A trapped-person detector is a sensitive machine that can pick up small vibrations. When trapped people try to move, they shake the rubble or broken bits of building or rock that lie around them. The small vibrations caused by this movement travel through the rubble.

The detector picks up the noise of any slight vibration. It makes the noise much louder electronically. A person's breathing can be detected. Rescuers wear headphones to hear the sounds of people that they could not hear otherwise.

A rescuer uses a trapped-person detector.

A rescue dog and its handler search earthquake rubble.

Where people cannot go into collapsed buildings, specially trained dogs often can. Dogs are excellent rescue animals. They have a keen sense of smell. They can sniff to find people who are trapped without being able to see or hear them.

Dogs have another advantage over people as rescuers. They weigh less than people. This means they can walk on rubble that might collapse if a heavier person walked on it.

A dog is trained to bark loudly when it smells a person. Then the rescue people know where they have to go to get a person out.

There is a lot of work to be done to help people who have been rescued from an earthquake or any other disaster. Many people no longer have homes, food, or water. Several organizations from around the world, such as the Red Cross, help these people. They bring people medical care, food and water, and help in the rebuilding of homes.

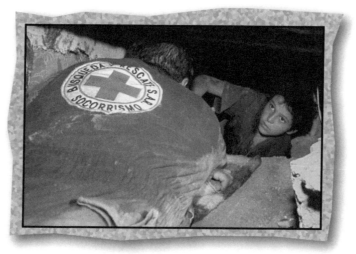

A Red Cross worker rescues a boy.

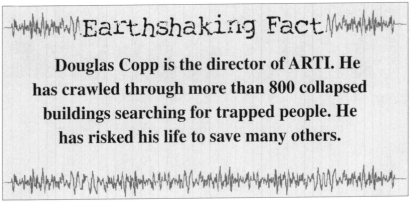

Earthshaking Fact

Douglas Copp is the director of ARTI. He has crawled through more than 800 collapsed buildings searching for trapped people. He has risked his life to save many others.

Chapter 6

Predicting Earthquakes

On a February night in 1983, a woman in Long Beach, California, woke up suddenly. She heard a strange sound. The birds were chirping loudly, even though it was the middle of the night.

Dogs often howl just before an earthquake happens.

The woman went back to sleep. An hour later she woke up again. This time the ground was shaking. It was an earthquake!

Did the birds start chirping in the middle of the night because they knew an earthquake was coming? It may be so. People all around the world have told stories of animals that acted strangely just before an earthquake happened.

Farmers and ranchers say that cows and horses often suddenly break through fences and run around wildly before an earthquake. People living in towns have noticed that cats and dogs suddenly leave their houses. They dash down the street, away from dangerous buildings. It was reported that dogs howled all night before the 1906 earthquake in San Francisco.

In China it is said that pandas moan before an earthquake. People who live near the coast in Japan talk about fish acting strangely. Just before a big earthquake the fish flop out of the water.

Can animals tell when earthquakes are about to happen? It seems to make sense that some animals may feel the very slight tremors that come before a big earthquake. Although animals may be able to sense earthquakes before people can, they can do little to warn people in time to run to safety.

Understanding why earthquakes happen has helped people work on predicting, or telling in advance, when an earthquake might happen. Seismologists are scientists who study earthquakes. They try to predict when and where earthquakes will occur. They use modern machines to measure very slight movements in the earth's crust.

One of the machines they use is called a creep meter. It measures the very slow movements of the earth's crust along faults. These movements are far too slight for people to feel, but they can sometimes be the early signs of an earthquake.

Seismologists also use laser beams. These can sense tiny movements of the earth's crust. Machines that use laser beams can show when the earth's crust has moved just one twenty-fifth of an inch.

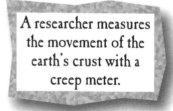

A researcher measures the movement of the earth's crust with a creep meter.

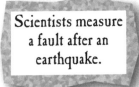
Scientists measure a fault after an earthquake.

Seismologists spend a lot of time studying fault lines and other places where earthquakes have already happened. When they find that the earth's crust is moving even slightly, they may warn that another earthquake might be coming. Then people can prepare their homes or leave for a safer place.

Earthquake prediction has saved many lives. However, the timing of most earthquakes is very hard to predict. Even the location of some earthquakes surprises scientists.

Three powerful earthquakes struck the state of Missouri in 1811 and 1812. Missouri is far from any major fault. It sits in the middle of a tectonic plate. Much later, scientists realized that there is a soft spot in the earth's crust under part of Missouri. The heat energy that built up under the earth's crust burst out of the soft spot and caused the earthquakes.

Scientists also look back at history to find patterns in the timing of earthquakes. If an area has had two major earthquakes in the past 200 years, scientists expect there's a good chance for earthquakes to happen there about every 100 years.

A part of the San Andreas fault in California seems to have been hit by earthquakes every 220 years. This area has not had a major earthquake in over 300 years. People worry that a big earthquake will happen at any time.

To find out when earthquakes have happened, scientists dig deep into the soil at a fault line. Places where layers of rock have been moved indicate an earthquake. Scientists can calculate the age of each layer of rock. The earthquake happened long ago if shifted rock is deep in the ground.

A scientist measures layers of rock.

Because earthquakes are so hard to predict, scientists cannot warn people before every earthquake. It is important for people to be prepared for an emergency. This is especially important for people who live in areas that are known to have earthquakes. If they can plan ahead, they will know what to do if they suddenly feel the earth shake.

Earthshaking Fact

Scientists may soon be able to predict earthquakes from space. Satellites can measure small changes along fault lines. They send the information to seismologists on Earth.

Chapter 7

Earthquake Safety

What should people do during an earthquake to stay safe? The most important thing people can do is to remain calm. Having an emergency earthquake plan helps people know what to do and feel less scared. Having a plan may even save lives.

Earthquake damage in a bookstore

Early one morning in 1994, a girl in Northridge, California, woke up when her bedroom dresser suddenly toppled over. In the darkness she heard the windows breaking and shelves falling. She knew it was an earthquake!

Although the girl was scared, she remembered her family's earthquake emergency plan. She found her little sister and stood with her and their mother in a doorway until the earthquake was over. Her quick action may have saved their lives!

Doorways are generally the strongest part of a house. Earthquake experts suggest that the doorways might remain steady even if the rest of the house is shaking. So people have a better chance of avoiding a falling wall or ceiling if they stay in a doorway during an earthquake.

A mother and her daughter show how to stand in a doorway during an earthquake.

People inside buildings should stay away from windows during an earthquake. The glass could break and scatter through the room and cause serious injuries. It is often advised that people get under a heavy table or bed. This gives some protection from falling objects, such as lamps and books. However, a piece of a ceiling may fall. If it is heavy enough to crush a table, getting under the table would not be a good thing to do.

A safer place, according to some experts, is next to a very sturdy object. A refrigerator and an upright piano are sturdy. A heavy piece of ceiling is less likely to crush these. Instead, the fallen material might create a "roof" over a space that is then protected.

People who are outside during an earthquake should move to an open place, like a field. They should stay away from buildings, power lines, and trees that might fall suddenly.

It is a good idea to keep an emergency kit ready for an earthquake or another sudden disaster. Possible supplies for a kit are bottled water, canned food, a flashlight, a battery-powered radio, and a fire extinguisher.

Schools in California have regular earthquake drills. These are a lot like fire drills in other schools. At a signal the children stop what they are doing and get under their desks.

In Japan and elsewhere, people learn what to do during an earthquake from special trucks that travel from town to town. Each truck carries a model room that can be made to shake as if there were an earthquake. People in the "room" act out what to do.

California children find out what an earthquake feels like in the "Shakey-Quakey Van" at the Museum of Science and Industry.

Today many people are working to plan ways for people to survive earthquakes. In Japan new buildings are specially designed with earthquakes in mind. Builders use steel and concrete in the walls of buildings to make them stronger and safer. Some buildings have special rubber and steel pads in their foundations. These will absorb the shaking during an earthquake. The tallest building in San Francisco, the Transamerica Pyramid, is built in a special way. It should remain standing during an earthquake.

The Transamerica Pyramid in San Francisco

Steel bars bend but don't break during an earthquake.

No person or technology can stop earthquakes from happening. No one can tell exactly when and where the next earthquake is going to happen. People learn to live with earthquakes by understanding them and preparing for them.

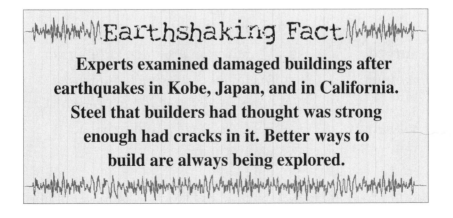

Earthshaking Fact

Experts examined damaged buildings after earthquakes in Kobe, Japan, and in California. Steel that builders had thought was strong enough had cracks in it. Better ways to build are always being explored.

Glossary

absorb   [ub ZORB] to take in and not reflect or throw back

avalanche   [AV uh lanch] large mass of snow, ice, or rocks that slides swiftly down a mountain

calculate   [KAL kyoo layt] to determine; to find out, often by using mathematics

destruction   [dihs TRUK shun] the act of breaking up, tearing down, ruining, or spoiling

focus   [FOH kus] a center of activity; the point where rays of sound, movement, heat, or light come together or a point from which they spread

rubble   [RUB ul] broken pieces from damaged buildings

scale   [skayl] a series of marks along a line, with regular spaces in between, used for measuring; a series of steps based on size or amount

surged   [surjd] moved in a sudden strong rush

tectonic   [tek TAHN ihk] relating to or caused by a break or shape in the earth's crust

vibrations   [vye BRAY shunz] rapid movements back and forth